31472400265835

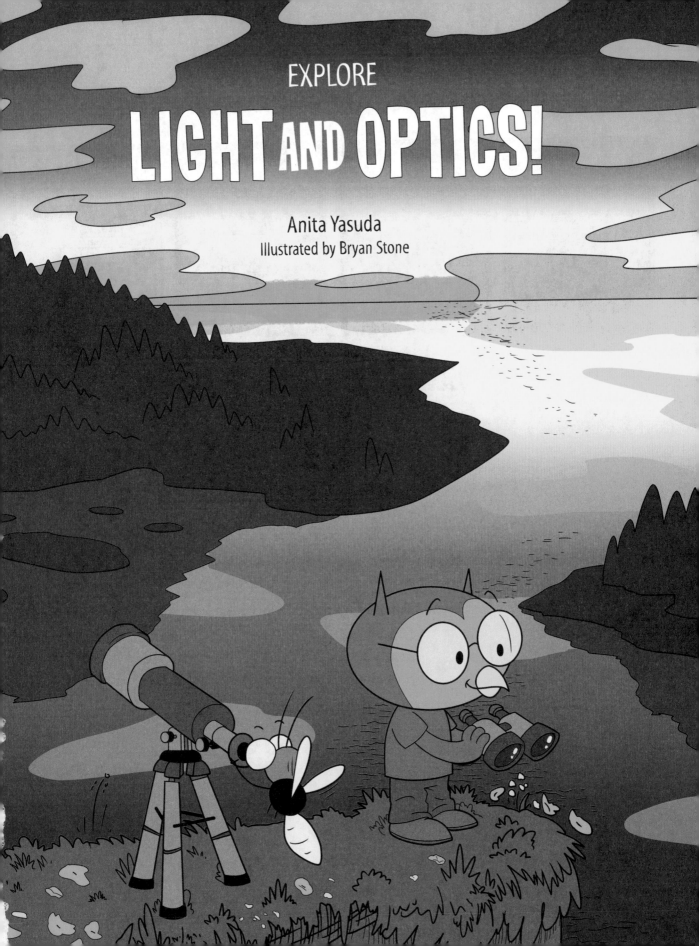

EXPLORE

LIGHT AND OPTICS!

Anita Yasuda

Illustrated by Bryan Stone

Recent science titles in the **Explore Your World!** Series

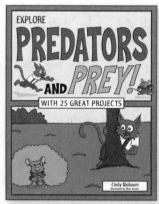

Check out more titles at www.nomadpress.net

Nomad Press
A division of Nomad Communications
10 9 8 7 6 5 4 3 2 1

This book was manufactured by Marquis Book Printing,
Montmagny, Québec, Canada
August 2016, Job #125544

ISBN Softcover: 978-1-61930-380-5
ISBN Hardcover: 978-1-61930-376-8

Educational Consultant, Marla Conn

Questions regarding the ordering of this book should be addressed to
Nomad Press
2456 Christian St.
White River Junction, VT 05001
www.nomadpress.net

Printed in Canada.

CONTENTS

Interested in primary sources? Look for this icon.
Use a smartphone or tablet app to scan the QR code and explore more!
You can find a list of URLs on the Resources page.

If the QR code doesn't work, try searching the Internet with
the Keyword Prompts to find other helpful sources.

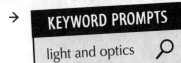

KEYWORD PROMPTS

light and optics

circa 300 BCE: The ancient Greeks believe light comes from the eye.

130 CE: Claudius Ptolemy publishes the book *Optics*.

1021 CE: Ibn al-Haytham, or Alhazen, describes the refraction of light.

1540–1559: Leonard Digges makes the first refracting telescope.

1590: Hans and Zacharias Janssen make the first microscope.

1604: Johannes Kepler publishes his findings on how the eye and lenses work in the *Optical Part of Astronomy*.

1608: Hans Lippershey invents a device that makes distant objects look closer.

1666: Isaac Newton describes how white light can be split into a spectrum.

1704: Isaac Newton publishes *Opticks*.

1727: James Bradley estimates the speed of light.

1792: William Murdoch pioneers the use of natural gas for lighting and heating.

1800: Sir Frederick William Herschel discovers infrared light.

1801: Johann Ritter finds ultraviolet light.

1826: Joseph Niépce creates the first photographic image.

1839: Louis Daguerre demonstrates to the public the daguerreotype method for producing photographs.

1854: John Tyndall shows that light can be bent.

1864: James Clerk Maxwell publishes his electromagnetic theory of light.

1878: Sir Joseph Wilson Swan patents a light bulb that uses a carbon paper filament.

1878: Albert Abraham Michelson measures the speed of light with great accuracy.

1879: Thomas Edison demonstrates his incandescent light bulb.

1887: Heinrich Hertz proves James Clerk Maxwell's electromagnetic theory.

1888: George Eastman invents the Kodak camera.

1895: Wilhelm Conrad Röntgen uses electromagnetic radiation to create the first X-ray.

1900: George Eastman launches the inexpensive Box Brownie camera, making photography accessible to more people.

1900–1933: Albert Einstein and Max Planck explain that light is both a wave and a particle.

1926: John Logie Baird invents a mechanical television system.

1927: Philo T. Farnsworth demonstrates an electronic television.

1931: Max Knott and Ernst Ruska invent the first electron microscope. In 1933, Ernst Ruska builds the first electron microscope.

1947: Dennis Gabor invents holography.

1954: Charles Townes and Arthur Schawlow invent the maser (microwave amplification by stimulated emission of radiation).

1960: Theodore Maiman demonstrates a working laser.

1966: Charles Kao and George Hockham demonstrate that optical fiber can transmit signals.

1990: The Hubble Space Telescope becomes the world's first space telescope.

2001: A pill-sized camera contained in a capsule is developed.

2003: Researchers at Tokyo University create optical camouflage.

2005: Scientists at the University of Berkeley develop a superlens with a resolution of 60 nanometers.

2018: The James Webb Space Telescope is set to be launched this year.

v

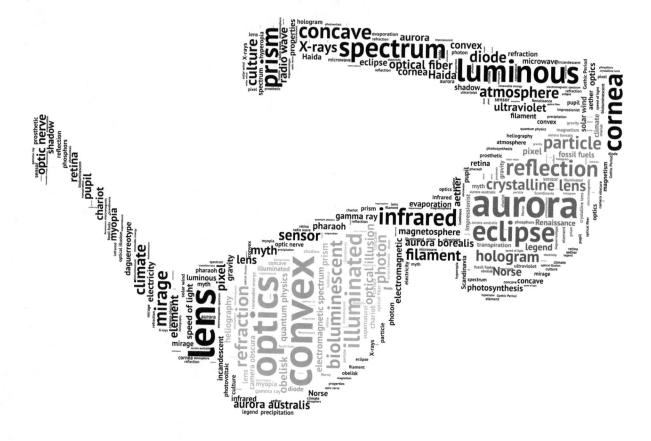

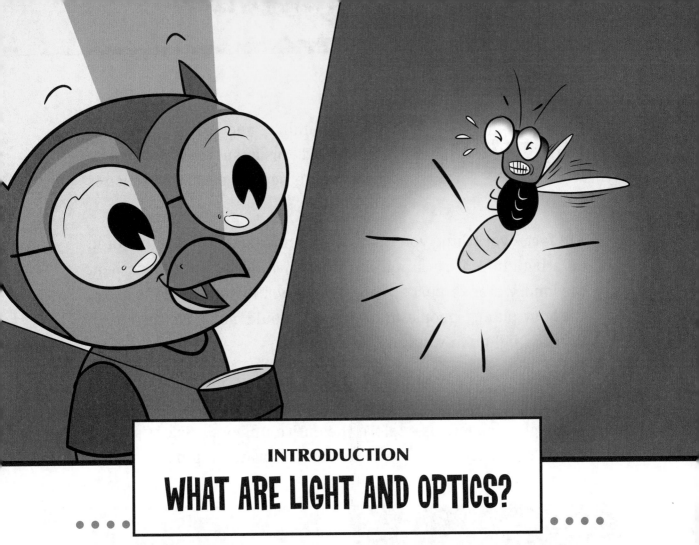

INTRODUCTION
WHAT ARE LIGHT AND OPTICS?

• • • •   • • • •

I spy with my little eye something that we can't live without. Plants and humans need it. It bounces and bends. It can become heat. It travels through air and water. It's faster than anything in the known universe. And some animals create their own. Have you guessed what it is? I spy light!

• •

What would happen if there was no light? Would you be able to see? Would there be food to eat? Close your eyes and think about a world with no light. What kinds of things would be impossible to do? What would happen if the sun, our biggest source of light, was gone? The world would be much different!

atmosphere: the blanket of air surrounding the earth.

WORDS TO KNOW

You wouldn't need a soccer ball, snowboard, or a surfboard because there would be no weather or seasons to enjoy.

In fact, everything you know would not exist. The earth would be a big lump of rock and ice. There would be nothing to heat the land, water, or atmosphere. Plants would not be able to grow. Without plants, people and animals would not have any food. Without light, we wouldn't be here!

Light makes many things possible every day. Special equipment uses light so we can investigate objects too small for our eyes to see. Light also lets us explore the entire universe. Scientists are using light science to find new ways of protecting our health.

Some objects actually produce light. Objects that make their own light are said to be luminous. The sun and fire are luminous objects. Some animals and insects, such as fireflies, create their own light. Objects that do not produce light but are lit up, such as mirrors, are said to be illuminated.

We communicate with light by using visible light to read books and newspapers. Do you ever use the Internet? Scientists found a way to send light over optical fibers. This makes it possible to talk to friends, watch videos, and discover new websites—all because of light!

luminous: describes an object that gives out its own light.

illuminated: describes an object that can reflect light to our eyes.

optical fiber: glass or plastic threads that transmit information in the form of light.

optics: the science of visible and invisible light.

WORDS TO KNOW

THE HISTORY OF LIGHT

Light makes many things possible, but what exactly is it? Can you hold it in your hands? Can you taste it or smell it? Is light something you can store in a drawer to use later? Scientists have been trying to answer questions like these for thousands of years.

The study of light is called optics. Centuries ago, people wanted to know why they could see in the daytime and not at nighttime. They made observations about how light worked and designed experiments to test light in different ways.

BCE: put after a date, BCE stands for Before Common Era and counts years down to zero. CE stands for Common Era and counts years up from zero. This book was published in 2016 CE.

properties: the unique characteristics of something.

eclipse: when a planet or other body in space is hidden by another body in space.

WORDS TO KNOW

The ancient Greeks were some of the earliest people to study optics. Ancient Greeks believed in many gods and goddesses. Around 450 BCE, a philosopher named Empedocles thought that our eyes contained light rays that shone out and let people see. He believed that the goddess Aphrodite made eyes from earth, water, air, and fire, and that it was the fire that made it possible for eyes to emit light rays. That makes people sound like superheroes!

LIGHT FROM THE TOP AND BOTTOM OF THE FIREFLY TRAVEL AT STRAIGHT ANGLES THROUGH THE HOLE TO THE OTHER SIDE OF THE WALL, WHERE THEY SWITCH TO BOTTOM AND TOP, SINCE THE LIGHT CAN'T BEND AROUND THE EDGES OF THE HOLE.

People believed this theory for nearly 1,500 years. Beginning in the 700s CE, the Middle East became a thriving center of learning. Scholars came to study astronomy, geometry, and other sciences.

One scholar called Alhazen thought a lot about light. He did many experiments to test his theories and study the properties of light. Have you ever seen an eclipse? This is when the moon and the sun line up with our planet and one blocks the light of the other.

ALHAZEN

Over his lifetime, Alhazen published nearly 100 books. In 1040, his *Book of Optics* was translated into Latin. It contained the laws of reflection and refraction. It described how he used experiments to test his hypotheses. This process would develop into the scientific method. Alhazen's book influenced European scholars for hundreds of years. You can learn more about Alhazen here.

KEYWORD PROMPTS

1001 inventions Ibn al-Haytham 🔍

reflection: when light hits an object and bounces off it.

refraction: when the direction of light changes.

shadow: a dark area created when light is blocked by an object.

lens: a piece of curved glass that can bend light to form an image that appears larger or smaller than the original object.

gravity: a physical force that pulls objects toward the center of the earth.

particle: a very tiny part of something.

WORDS TO KNOW

Alhazen wanted to know more about eclipses, sunsets, and shadows. Alhazen experimented with mirrors and lenses. He studied how light traveled through a tiny opening into a darkened room. This way, he proved that light does not come from the eye, but enters into the eye.

LIGHT ARGUMENTS

People still wanted to learn more about light. In the late 1600s, English scientist Isaac Newton began investigating the properties of light. Newton was already famous for discovering the laws of gravity and motion. Newton came to believe that light was made of very small particles he called corpuscles that travel in a straight line. Newton also discovered that white light is actually made of different colors.

aether: an unknown material that some people once believed filled space.

WORDS TO KNOW

A Dutch scientist named Christiaan Huygens thought light was made of waves. He published his theory in 1690. He believed that, like waves in the sea, light waves move through space, which was thought to be filled with a mysterious substance called aether.

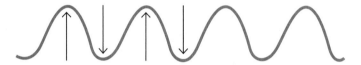

LIGHT WAVES MOVE UP AND DOWN THROUGH AETHER

Which theory do you think was right, particles or waves? People around the world debated this question for many years.

In 1801, an English scientist named Thomas Young did an experiment with light. He aimed a ray of light toward a wall through a piece of cloth with two slits cut into it. If the light was made of particles, he thought, then it should appear as two lines of light on the wall. If the light was made of waves, it would appear as many lines of light and dark because of the way waves move. What did Young see? Many lines of light and dark—waves!

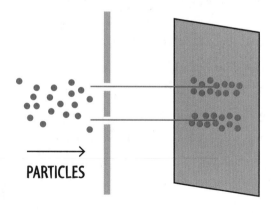

PARTICLES

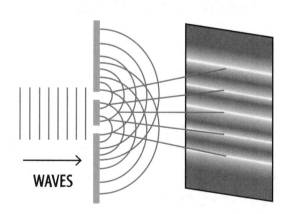

WAVES

The debate wasn't quite over, however. In the 1900s, a physicist name Albert Einstein did many experiments with light and showed that we could think of light as both a particle and a wave. A photon is a tiny burst of energy that travels in waves. Photons are both a particle and a wave. This was such a different way of thinking that a new branch of science was established, called quantum physics.

It's easy to think there is only one type of light wave, the light you can see, but there are actually lots of different kinds of light waves. Visible light is the only type of energy that human eyes can see.

PS It wasn't until 2015, when scientists took an historic photograph, that anyone was able to observe light in both particle and wave form at the same time. **See the photo and read about the process here.**

KEYWORD PROMPTS

light wave particle photograph 🔍

JOHANNES KEPLER

MEET A LIGHT PIONEER!

Have you ever created shadow puppets on the wall? We don't know if Johannes Kepler (1571–1630) played this game, but in 1604, he published a book on light. In it, he explained how light travels in straight lines, how it can be bent, and how a shadow is created when the ray of light is blocked.

electricity: a form of energy that results from the interaction of electrically charged particles.

magnetism: the attracting and repelling force that results from the motion of electrically charged particles.

electromagnetic: one of the fundamental forces of the universe, which is responsible for magnetic attraction and electrical charges.

electromagnetic spectrum: the entire range of electromagnetic waves.

WORDS TO KNOW

DIFFERENT TYPES OF LIGHT WAVES

In 1864, Scottish mathematician, James Clerk Maxwell showed the link between electricity and magnetism. He proved that light was made of electromagnetic waves, which produce magnetism. Have you ever used magnets? The waves that cause the magnets to attract and repel each other are light waves.

Scientists call the entire range of light the electromagnetic spectrum. Each wave on the electromagnetic spectrum has a different wavelength that can be used for different things.

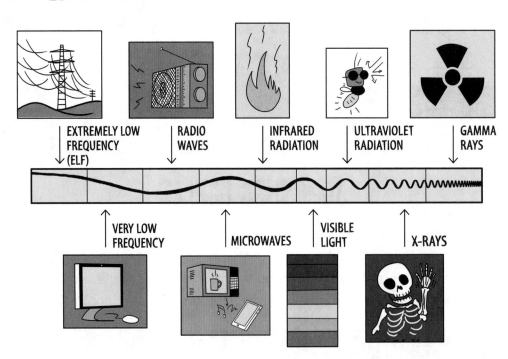

EXTREMELY LOW FREQUENCY (ELF)   RADIO WAVES   INFRARED RADIATION   ULTRAVIOLET RADIATION   GAMMA RAYS

VERY LOW FREQUENCY   MICROWAVES   VISIBLE LIGHT   X-RAYS

The longest waves on the spectrum are radio waves. They can be larger than the earth! At the opposite end are short gamma rays. Radio waves are used to carry information to televisions and radios.

Microwaves are used for many activities such as communications and cooking. Appliances such as toasters, security systems, and your television remote use infrared light waves. Hospitals use ultraviolet rays to kill germs. Doctors use X-rays to see inside the body and gamma rays to kill cancer cells. What kinds of light rays have you used today?

THE SPEED OF LIGHT

Have you ever ridden on a roller coaster? While roller coasters are fast, the speed of light is a lot faster. Photons whip along at 186,000 miles per second! That's fast, but people used to think light went a lot faster. They thought light moved instantly.

spectrum: in optics, a separation of color.

radio wave: an electromagnetic wave used to transmit radio and television signals and for navigation.

gamma ray: short electromagnetic waves.

microwave: an electromagnetic wave that we use to heat food.

infrared: an invisible type of light with a longer wavelength than visible light, which can also be felt as heat.

ultraviolet: a kind of light with short wavelengths. It can't be seen with the naked eye.

X-rays: radiation that allows doctors to see your bones.

speed of light: the speed at which light travels, which is 186,000 miles per second.

WORDS TO KNOW

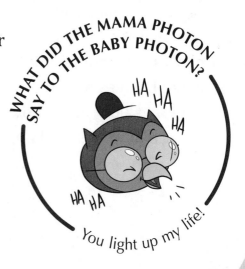

WHAT DID THE MAMA PHOTON SAY TO THE BABY PHOTON?

HA HA HA HA HA

You light up my life!

In 1638, Galileo, an Italian astronomer and mathematician, tried to measure the speed of light. Galileo and his assistant took lanterns to the tops of two mountains. His assistant flashed the lantern and Galileo tried to time how long it took to see it.

Unfortunately, the experiment didn't work. Galileo didn't have the technology to measure microseconds. But he still knew that light traveled extremely fast.

It wasn't until 1676 that the speed of light was accurately measured. A Danish astronomer named Ole Rømer measured light by timing the eclipses of Jupiter's moon, Io. From these measurements, he was able to figure out that the speed of light is 186,000 miles per second. If you could travel at the speed of light, you could zoom around the earth almost eight times in one second!

In this book, you will investigate the important role light plays in your life. You'll read what light is, how it works, and how our eyes are built to see it. You'll discover why the sky is blue and how a rainbow is created. You'll also learn how the science of optics is changing the way we live.

GOOD SCIENCE PRACTICES

Every good scientist keeps a science journal! Choose a notebook to use as your science journal. As you read through this book and do the activities, keep track of your observations in a scientific method worksheet, like the one shown here. Scientists use the scientific method to keep their experiments organized.

Step	Example
1. Question: What are we trying to find out? What problem are we trying to solve?	Is it easier to see in the dark or with light?
2. Research: What knowledge do we already have?	Other people say it's easier to see in the light.
3. Hypothesis/Prediction: What do we think the answer will be?	I think it's easier to see in the daytime.
4. Equipment: What supplies are we using?	This book, a flashlight, and a science journal.
5. Method: What procedure are we following?	When it's dark, turn off the lights in your room and try to read this book. Turn on your flashlight and try again.
6. Results: What happened and why?	It's probably easier for you to see with light!

Each chapter of this book begins with a question to help guide your exploration of light and optics. Keep the question in your mind as you read the chapter. At the end of each chapter, use your science journal to record your thoughts and answers.

 INVESTIGATE!

How do you think the ancient Greeks explained why people could not see in the dark?

HOW LIGHT TRAVELS

Scientists know that light travels very quickly. In this experiment, you will discover whether light really does travel in a straight line.

SUPPLIES

* science journal and pencil
* 4 index cards
* hole puncher
* red marker
* modeling clay
* 12-inch ruler
* dark room
* flashlight

1 Before you begin, start a scientific method worksheet in your science journal. What is your hypothesis about how light travels?

2 Punch a hole through the center of three of the index cards. The hole must be in the same spot for all three cards.

3 Place one of these index cards over the fourth card and trace the hole onto it with a pencil.

THEN & NOW

THEN: The ancient Greeks believed that fire came from the gods. A god named Prometheus stole fire from the home of the gods on Mount Olympus and gave it to humans. He was severely punished for this.

NOW: We know that fire is a reaction between oxygen and a fuel, such as wood. But the world hasn't forgotten Prometheus. At the beginning of each Olympic Games, a burning torch is brought from Greece to the country hosting the games in commemoration of the theft of fire.

4 Color the circle on the fourth index card with the red marker.

5 Put a small piece of clay at the bottom of each card to make them stand upright.

6 Space the cards 10 inches apart using the ruler. The card with the red dot will be the last one in the line.

7 Turn off the lights and turn on the flashlight. Standing directly in front of the first card, shine the flashlight through the hole. What do you observe? Do your results support or not support your hypothesis?

TRY THIS! Hold the flashlight at different angles. Does this change the way the light travels through the holes? How?

PROJECT!

TRACKING THE SUN'S MOVEMENTS

SUPPLIES
* science journal
* pencil

Ancient astronomers built observatories to track the sun. In this activity, you will study the movements of the sun.

1 Create a 3-column chart with 16 rows. Label the columns with *Month - Week*, *Sunrise*, and *Sunset*.

KEYWORD PROMPTS

time and date 🔍

2 Record the sunrise and sunset at the beginning of each new week during a course of three months. Use a local resource such as a television channel or newspaper. With an adult's permission, you can visit this website for more information.

Month - Week	Sunrise	Sunset
August - 1	7:03 am	8:45 pm
August - 2	7:08 am	8:42 pm
August - 3	7:13 am	8:35 pm
August - 4	7:18 am	8:25 pm

PROJECT!

3 Using your data, make a graph showing the differences in sunrise and sunset during the three months.

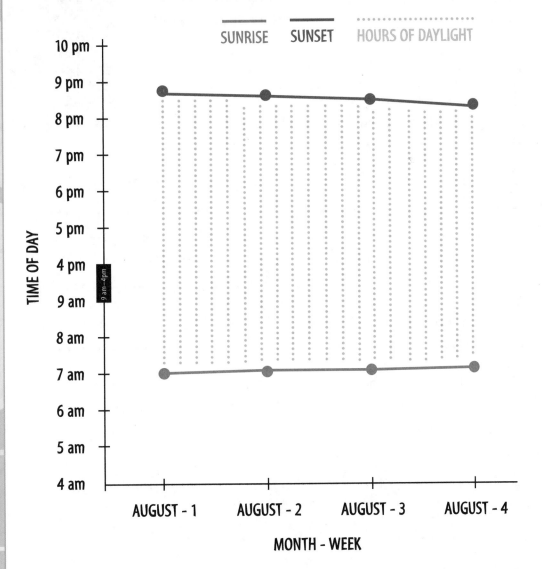

SUNRISE SUNSET HOURS OF DAYLIGHT

TIME OF DAY

10 pm
9 pm
8 pm
7 pm
6 pm
5 pm
4 pm
9 am
8 am
7 am
6 am
5 am
4 am

AUGUST - 1 AUGUST - 2 AUGUST - 3 AUGUST - 4

MONTH - WEEK

THINK ABOUT IT: What does your graph tell you about the sun? Do you see any patterns? How could this data be useful? Think about how this information may have been useful to people long ago.

LIGHT ENCOUNTERS

Light passes through glass windows but not through solid brick walls. You are going to investigate a variety of objects to discover which ones allow light to pass through them.

SUPPLIES

* science journal and pencil
* clear glass cup
* clear sandwich bag
* wax paper
* tissue
* book
* tinfoil
* flashlight

1 In your notebook create two charts with three headings—Translucent, Transparent, and Opaque.

2 Assemble all the objects from the supplies list in front of you.

3 After examining each object, predict which category the object will be in. If you can see completely through an object, it is transparent. If you can see partially through an object, it is translucent. If you can't see through an object, it is opaque. Write the name of each object in the corresponding category on chart one.

4 To test your hypotheses, shine the flashlight on each object one at a time. Write the name of the object in the corresponding category on chart two.

5 Compare your two charts. Did your results correspond to your guesses? If not, what made you think differently?

THINK ABOUT IT: What makes an object transparent, translucent, or opaque? Are there any objects that fall into more than one of these categories?

CHAPTER 1
LIGHT FROM THE SUN

The brightest star in the sky is the sun. We need it for many things on Earth. The sun is the main source of energy for every living creature on our planet. It gives us light and keeps us warm. It powers the seasons and the planet's climate. Our climate system includes all the planet's land, air, water, ice, and living things.

For many thousands of years, people have used the sun's light and heat. They created traditions about it and explanations for how it came to be.

WORDS TO KNOW

climate: the average weather patterns in an area during a long period of time.

myth: a story about make-believe creatures that people once believed were real.

legend: a story that is partly based on a true historical event or person.

culture: the beliefs and behavior of a particular group of people.

Haida: a native group of people living mostly in the Pacific Northeast.

supernatural: beings, objects, or events that cannot be explained.

WORDS TO KNOW

INVESTIGATE!

How did ancient cultures show the importance of the sun to their survival? How do today's cultures show this?

Before science was developed enough to explain the structure of the sun, ancient peoples turned to myths and legends. For some cultures, the sun was a god racing across the sky. Others believed it to be a campfire lit daily to keep the people of the earth warm.

The Haida of the Pacific Northwest tell a story of the sky chief and the Raven. The sky chief once kept a special yellow ball that was the sun in a box. One day, the Raven stole the beautiful ball to bring light into the world.

Aboriginal tribes in Australia also believed that supernatural events created the sun. One of their stories tells of the Rainbow Serpent, which not only made the land, rivers, and lakes, but also the sun, fire, and colors.

THEN & NOW

THEN: The ancient Greeks used mirrors to direct the sun's rays into their homes to keep them warm.

NOW: Germany is a leader in using solar energy. The country's solar plants produce more than 6 percent of its electrical needs.

obelisk: a four-sided tapered stone tower.

pharaoh: the title for an ancient Egyptian king.

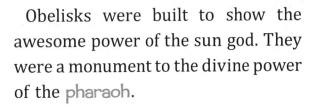

SUN WORSHIP

In some cultures, the sun was an important part of religious beliefs. From the Middle East to North America, people built temples and monuments in honor of it. Ancient Egyptians constructed massive, towering monuments called obelisks that were symbols of the sun god, Ra. A reflective metal that covered the top of an obelisk caught the first rays of light each morning.

Obelisks were built to show the awesome power of the sun god. They were a monument to the divine power of the pharaoh.

In Egypt, the pharaoh was thought of as a living god. Myths explaining the daily cycle of light and darkness tell of Ra and a crew of gods and goddesses sailing across the sky in a golden boat. At night, the journey continued in the underworld.

MEET A LIGHT PIONEER!

GALILEO GALILEI

Italian scientist and inventor Galileo Galilei (1564–1642) built his first telescope in 1609. He used it to study Earth's moon and four of Jupiter's moons. Based on his observations, Galileo determined that the planets rotate around the sun. Up until then, everyone thought the planets circled the earth.

chariot: a vehicle pulled by horses used by ancient Greeks and Romans for races and in battle.

Norse: people who lived in ancient Scandinavia.

Scandinavia: the countries of Sweden, Norway, Denmark, and Finland.

Aztecs: a Native American people who established an empire in central Mexico.

WORDS TO KNOW

Several cultures told stories about sun gods traveling across the sky. In India, legends tell of a sun god, Surya, who rides across the sky in a horse-drawn chariot. Greek myths speak of Apollo, a god who does the same thing. The Norse of Scandinavia imagined the sun and moon riding in chariots as evil wolves chased after them.

During the thirteenth century, the Aztecs in central Mexico worshiped Huitzilopochtli, god of the sun and war. The god's name means "hummingbird of the south." The Aztecs made daily human sacrifices to Huitzilopochtli because they believed that the god had to be fed daily!

WHAT HOLDS THE SUN UP IN THE SKY?

HA HA HA

HA HA

Sunbeams!

SURYA'S CHARIOT

In the thirteenth century, Indians built the temple of Konârak on the Bay of Bengal in the shape of Surya's chariot. The chariot is being pulled by seven horses, though only six remain today. The temple features 24 wheels carved with symbols for the seasons and months.

PS   Watch this UNESCO video on the temple.

KEYWORD PROMPTS

UNESCO sun temple video 🔍

SUN POWER

Today, scientists use telescopes and spacecraft to uncover the sun's secrets. The largest solar instrument in the world is found outside Tucson, Arizona. The McMath-Pierce Solar Telescope is 100 feet high and includes a 200-foot shaft that slants away from the telescope into the ground. It has been used to study the sun since 1962.

element: a pure substance whose atoms are all the same. It cannot be broken down into a simpler substance. Everything in the universe is made up of elements and combinations of elements. Oxygen, gold, hydrogen, and helium are elements.

WORDS TO KNOW

Researchers have learned a lot about the sun. The sun is a giant in our solar system. Almost 1,300,000 earths could fit inside it. Yet the sun is considered to be just average in size for a star.

Our sun is a burning globe of gases. These gases are 70 percent hydrogen, 28 percent helium, and 2 percent other elements. It might seem as though the sun never changes, but the hydrogen there is constantly converting into helium, which produces energy and light.

2% OTHER

28% HELIUM

70% HYDROGEN

It takes sunlight eight minutes to travel the 93,000,000 miles to the earth, even traveling at the incredible speed of 186,000 miles per second. Not all of this energy reaches us. Clouds and ice reflect some of the sun's light back into space. About 70 percent is absorbed by the earth's atmosphere, clouds, land, and sea.

photosynthesis: the process in which plants use light energy, carbon dioxide, and water to produce glucose and oxygen.

WORDS TO KNOW

PHOTOSYNTHESIS

The sun fuels nearly all life on the earth. Plants turn the sun's energy into food by a process called photosynthesis. The word comes from the Greek language meaning "light" and "put together." There are many steps and chemical reactions involved in photosynthesis.

Plants absorb water and minerals from the ground through their roots up to the leaves. During the day, the leaves collect energy from sunlight. Photons from the sun are absorbed by tiny cells on the green parts of a plant, such as its leaves or stem. These cells are like miniature factories where light, carbon dioxide, and water are combined to make glucose and oxygen. Carbon dioxide is a gas that plants get from the air. Glucose is a sugar that plants use for food.

Through photosynthesis, plants grow. Animals eat the plants, and we eat both plants and animals. That means, without the sun, life as we know it would not be here.

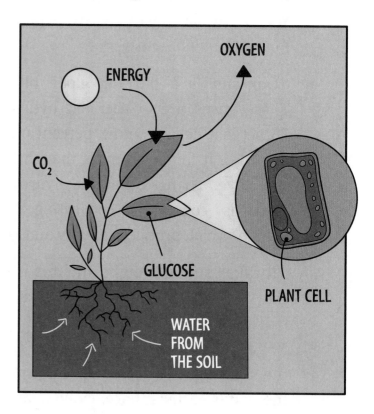

OXYGEN

ENERGY

CO_2

GLUCOSE

PLANT CELL

WATER FROM THE SOIL

THE WATER CYCLE

The earth's water moves from land and ocean to sky and back again in a process called the water cycle. Without the sun's energy, the water cycle would not work.

Water absorbs energy from the sun in a process called evaporation. When water evaporates, it changes from a liquid to a gas called water vapor. You cannot see water vapor because it is invisible. To understand how evaporation happens, think about the fact that water is made of incredibly tiny molecules. Each drop of water contains millions of molecules, but your eyes are not able to see them.

Water evaporates at all temperatures, but it speeds up as the temperature rises. This is because heat energy makes molecules move faster and faster. Some of those water molecules move fast enough to change from a liquid to a gas. Think about a rain puddle after a storm. The puddle does not stay on the ground forever. Some of this water seeps into the ground and some water molecules rise into the air as water vapor.

The world's oceans, seas, lakes, and rivers provide 90 percent of the water vapor in the atmosphere. Some water also moves into the air through the leaves of plants and trees. This process is called transpiration.

evaporation: the process of a liquid heating up and changing into a gas, such as water vapor.

molecule: a very small particle made of combinations of atoms.

transpiration: the process by which a plant pulls water up through its roots, which then collects on its leaves and evaporates into the atmosphere.

WORDS TO KNOW

Did You Know?

If all the water vapor fell at the same time, it would cover the earth with only 1 inch of water.

23

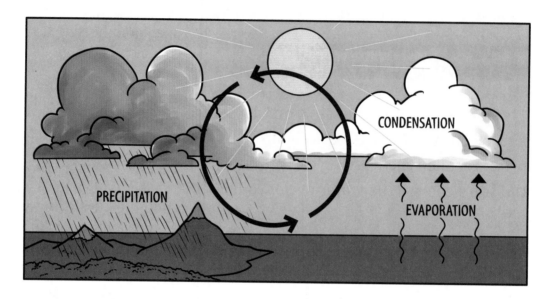

Once in the air, the wind spreads the water vapor throughout the atmosphere. Water vapor doesn't stay in the air very long. Within several days, it cools to form tiny droplets. This is called condensation. The tiny droplets fall to Earth as precipitation. The temperature decides whether this precipitation falls as rain, sleet, or snow.

Most precipitation collects in the oceans because oceans cover more than 70 percent of our planet. Some precipitation flows off the land into lakes, rivers, and streams. Water that sinks into the ground becomes groundwater. And the process begins again. The water cycle wouldn't be possible without the light from the sun!

WORDS TO KNOW

condensation: the process of a gas cooling down and changing into a liquid.

precipitation: water in the air in any form, such as snow, hail, or rain, that falls to the ground.

? INVESTIGATE!

It's time to consider and discuss: How did ancient cultures show the importance of the sun to their survival? How do today's cultures show this?

PROJECT!

SUN MYTHS

SUPPLIES
* paper and pencil
* ruler

In this activity, you will research sun myths from two different cultures. With the help of an adult, use appropriate online sites or books from your library. You can find useful information at these sites.

1 Create a chart. Fold a sheet of printer paper in half lengthways. Gently press along the seam and unfold. Use your ruler to draw a line along the crease. Now divide the paper horizontally into four even spaces.

KEYWORD PROMPTS

teacher scholastic myths
American folklore myths

2 Go online or to a library and research two sun myths. One should be from a Native American tribe.

3 Write the name of each myth at the top of the chart. Write your answers to these questions on the chart.

- Who created the sun in the myths?

- How was the sun placed in the sky?

- If humans or animals were part of the story, what was their relationship to the sun?

4 For the last space, draw a picture for each myth. Think about how the myths are the same. How are they different?

TRY THIS! You can try making up your myth about how the sun formed. Share your myth with a friend.

MEASURING THE SPEED OF LIGHT

Galileo had to travel to a hilltop to try to measure the speed of light. You can measure the speed of light in your kitchen. Have an adult help you with the microwave.

SUPPLIES

* science journal and pencil
* large microwavable plate
* 3 to 4 processed cheese slices
* microwave
* metric ruler

1 Before you begin the experiment, start a scientific method worksheet in your science journal. What is your hypothesis about what will happen to the cheese slices when they are put in the microwave? Why?

2 Remove the spinning plate from inside the microwave and place to one side.

3 Place one layer of cheese slices on a microwavable dinner plate.

4 Place the plate with the cheese inside the microwave and heat on low until just melted. Watch carefully.

5 Take the plate out of the microwave. There should be spots where the cheese melted and areas where it didn't melt. Take the ruler and measure the shortest distance between the hot spots in centimeters. Record this number in your journal.

6 This number is the measurement of half a wavelength. You will have to multiply this number by two to discover the length of an entire wavelength. Write this number down.

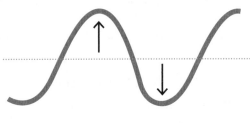

measurement × 2 = wavelength

___ centimeters × 2 = ___ centimeters wavelength

7 Look on the back of your microwave or in the manual to discover its frequency. Most microwaves operate at 2,450 megahertz, or 2,450,000,000 hertz.

8 To find the speed of light, multiply the frequency (2,450,000,000) by the wavelength.

Frequency of microwave × wavelength (distance between hotspots × 2) = ___ centimeters per second (speed of light)

2,450,000,000 hertz × ___ centimeters = ___ centimeters per second

9 The speed of light is usually given in meters. The actual speed of light is 299,792,458 meters/second. To convert your answer to meters, divide it by 100. Were your calculations close?

TRY THIS! Try this experiment with different food, such as chocolate or egg whites. Try measuring the distance between several heat spots. Do you come up with similar answers each time?

THE PROCESS OF PHOTOSYNTHESIS

You are always breathing in oxygen and releasing carbon dioxide. You can tell people are breathing by watching their chests move up and down as their lungs expand and deflate. In this experiment, you will observe how a leaf breathes.

1 Start a scientific method worksheet. What do you think will happen to the leaf when it is put under the water? Why? Write your hypothesis in your science journal.

2 Fill the jug with hot water. Place the leaf in the jug.

3 Over the next four hours, watch your leaf and write down your observations in your science journal. Was you hypothesis correct? Did anything about your experiment surprise you?

WHAT'S HAPPENING? During transpiration, the leaf expels water vapor and oxygen through tiny holes called the stomata. What do you see forming on the leaf when it's underwater? Why? Did one side have more air bubbles than the other? If so, can you think of a reason for this? Do you think your experiment would turn out differently if you used cold water? Why or why not? Try it!

MAKE AN OBELISK

In ancient Egypt, obelisks held commanding positions at the entrance to temples. Now it is your turn to design and create a paper obelisk.

1 Lay the paper or cardboard flat on a table.

2 Using your ruler and pencil, draw a row of four 2-by-9-inch pencil-like shapes for the obelisk. Between each shape, draw a dotted line to represent the fold line. Add a quarter inch to one end for the last fold.

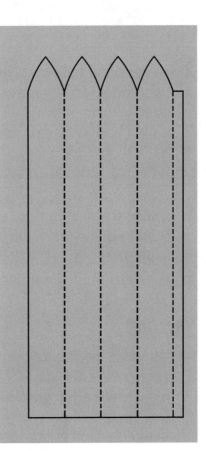

3 Carefully cut around the entire drawing. On each shape, write down one fact that you have learned about the sun from this chapter or draw a picture about this fact.

4 Next, press along the fold lines to form the obelisk. Glue the last fold to the first. If you want, create a square base for the obelisk from extra craft paper. Display your obelisk in your room.

CREATE A MINI WATER CYCLE

The earth's water is always changing between a liquid and a gas and a solid. In this experiment, you can observe the change that happens between a liquid and a gas.

1 Place the dirt with grass at the bottom of your container. Next to the dirt, create a mini pond out of the foil.

2 Fill the pond halfway with water. Spray the sod with water and put the lid back on the container

3 Place the container by a window that receives a lot of sunlight.

4 In your science journal, write down your observations. What happens to the sod? To the pond? What happens on the sides of the container?

TRY THIS!

* Measure the amount of water in your pond each day. Graph your results into a bar graph. You can use this site to present your findings: nces.ed.gov/nceskids/createagraph.

* Create a second experiment by placing your container in a shady location. Compare your results.

CHAPTER 2
COLOR PLAY

Have you ever seen a light show where laser beams create awesome patterns for the audience to enjoy? Nature also creates fantastic visual events in the sky, including mirages, rainbows, auroras, sunrises, and sunsets. In this chapter, you will even learn about light shows put on by plants and animals.

You can see the sky change simply by looking at it. There's an old rhyme that goes, "Red sky at night, sailor's delight. Red sky in morning, sailor's warning." Why does the sky look blue on a bright day and change to red and orange and pink as the sun sets?

Light from the sun travels through our atmosphere. The atmosphere is made up of five layers that are thicker the closer they are to the earth. Light collides with small particles in the atmosphere, such as oxygen and nitrogen molecules, dust, and tiny droplets of water.

Light bounces off these particles in all directions. This process is called scattering. The amount of scattering depends on the wavelength of the light. Short wavelengths scatter more than longer wavelengths.

Violet light, followed by blue, has the shortest wavelengths. The sky looks blue and not violet to our eyes because we are more sensitive to blue light. So on clear days, the sky looks blue because blue light scatters more than red light.

INVESTIGATE!

If light contains all colors, then why does a blue bike look blue?

prism: a solid, often made of glass, that is used to split light.

WORDS TO KNOW

The same scattering process happens at sunrise and sunset. When the sun is closer to the horizon, its light travels through more of the atmosphere to reach your eyes than it does when the sun is overhead. Shorter wavelengths such as blue and green are almost entirely scattered away. The long red wavelengths that pass through are what our eyes see.

BENDING WHITE LIGHT

Long ago, people thought that light was colorless. Just as artists make colors on their palette by mixing paints, people thought objects, such as crystals, colored light. In the seventeenth century, British scientist Isaac Newton wanted to know more about color. In 1664, he began experimenting with a triangular glass shape called a prism.

Holding the prism by a window, Newton succeeded in splitting sunlight into a line of different colors called a spectrum. When light enters a prism, it slows down, causing the light to disperse. Different wavelengths disperse at different speeds, making different colors! Newton used a lens and a second prism to recombine the colors. Newton's experiments with prisms were important. They showed that light was made of colors.

LIGHT →

LIGHT

GLASS PRISM

Learn more about Newton at this website.

KEYWORD PROMPTS

The Newton Project 🔍

RAINBOWS

Water droplets in the sky, near a waterfall, or even on a spider's web act like prisms to create rainbows. Several cultures have seen the rainbow's candy-colored arc as a bridge between the earth and sky. The Navajo and the Norse believed a rainbow connected the earth to lands where their gods lived.

In India, people saw the multicolored arc as strings on the god Indra's bow. According to myth, Indra used his bow to shoot arrows of lightning.

One of the most popular rainbow tales comes from Ireland. Folktales tell of magical creatures called leprechauns who hid their pots of gold at the ends of rainbows.

Sadly, you can't walk across a rainbow, and you won't find a pot of gold at the end either. A rainbow is made of sunlight. It appears after sunlight travels through water droplets—trillions of them.

WHAT DID ONE FIREFLY SAY TO THE OTHER?

HA HA HA HA HA

You light up my life!

Raindrops act as tiny prisms. They refract the sunlight, which slows down as it passes through the water. Some light is reflected off the droplets. As light leaves the droplets, it is bent again, separating the wavelengths. Your eyes are then able to see the colors of a rainbow.

aurora borealis: the northern lights.

aurora australis: the southern lights.

WORDS TO KNOW

AURORAS

An aurora is a natural display of shimmering colors in the night sky, generally seen in the far north or the far south of the earth. In the north, the aurora is called the northern lights. In the south, the aurora is called the southern lights.

More than 30,000 years ago, people in southern France drew pictures of what might be the northern lights on cave walls. Much later, people tried to explain the lights in stories. In Labrador, shimmering patches of light were thought to be torches held by spirits guiding souls. The Inuit of Greenland believed the lights were a ball game being played by spirits running across the heavens. In Finland, people told a tale of sparks flying off the tail of an arctic fox as it touched the mountains.

It wasn't until 1621 that French astronomer Pierre Gassendi would give these ribbons of light the names we now use. He called the northern lights the aurora borealis for Aurora, the Roman goddess of dawn. Boreas was the Roman god of the north wind. In the Southern Hemisphere, south of the equator, they are called the aurora australis, or southern lights.

MEET A LIGHT PIONEER!

JOHANN WILHELM RITTER

In 1801, German physicist Johann Wilhelm Ritter (1776–1810) discovered an area of the spectrum that no one knew existed. While conducting experiments with a silver nitrate solution, he found light beyond the purple end of the visible spectrum. Ritter's discovery became known as ultraviolet light.

An aurora does not begin here on the earth. It begins millions of miles away with the red-hot ball of gas we call the sun.

The outer layer of the sun is made of electrically charged particles. Some of the charged particles are so energetic that the sun's gravity is not able to hold on to them. These high-speed particles stream into space. The stream is called the solar wind.

The solar wind travels at a rate of more than a million miles per hour. Though this is incredibly fast, it still takes the wind four days to travel the 93 million miles to the earth. The solar wind then encounters the earth's magnetic shield, which is called the magnetosphere. The magnetosphere deflects most of the solar wind away from the earth.

Some of the particles ride along the earth's magnetic field to the magnetic poles. The particles strike oxygen and nitrogen in the earth's upper atmosphere. These collisions decide the color of the aurora. Oxygen leads to green and red auroras. Nitrogen gives off a mix of blue and red that turns the sky a deep purple.

While we are only able to see the aurora at night, it happens during the day, too. Scientists are tracking and studying the aurora to learn more about what causes it. They want to know how we might control it, and whether it's useful for anything.

PS To learn more about the aurora, visit this NASA page.

KEYWORD PROMPTS

NASA aurora video 🔍

MIRAGES

Did You Know?

Have you ever been riding in a car on a hot, sunny day and noticed that the ground up ahead looks wet? What happens when you reach the wet part? It disappears! You were seeing a mirage!

In 1818, explorer John Ross set out from Britain to discover the Northwest Passage between the Atlantic and Pacific Oceans. At the time, people wanted to find a faster route to the Far East from Europe. Explorers searched the Arctic Ocean for a route connecting the Atlantic and Pacific Oceans.

During his voyage, Ross encountered a towering mountain range near Baffin Island, Canada. Believing that the mountains blocked his route, Ross returned home. It was later discovered that the mountain range was a mirage!

A mirage is an optical illusion. Light travels in a straight line to your eye, but temperature affects the speed of light. On a hot day, the ground absorbs heat. It radiates this heat to the air above. But the layer of air above this is not as warm. When sunlight passes between the two layers, it is refracted. The light rays bend upward. Your eyes do not see the bend. We are tricked into thinking that it traveled in a straight line from an object on the ground!

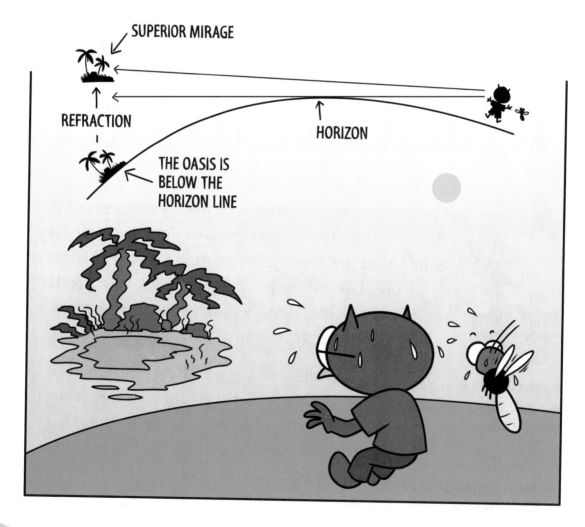

SUPERIOR MIRAGE

REFRACTION

HORIZON

THE OASIS IS BELOW THE HORIZON LINE

bioluminescent: when living things give off light by hosting a chemical reaction in their bodies.

WORDS TO KNOW

The mirage that explorer Ross saw is called a superior mirage. It occurs when there is a layer of cold air beneath warmer air. The light passes through these layers and is bent toward the eye. Objects can appear to float on the horizon. They might look higher or nearer than they actually are.

People often see mirages in deserts, because mirages are most common in hot areas. A desert mirage happens when light rays bend as they travel through layers of cool air to the extremely hot air near the sand. When the light bends, the blue sky and the white clouds appear as if they are real objects on the sand. It is easy to think there is a pool of water instead of a reflection of the sky.

INVESTIGATE!

It's time to consider and discuss: If light contains all colors, then why does a blue bike look blue?

LIGHT AND LIVING ORGANISMS

There are many types of living things that create their own light, including fish, insects, and plants. Creatures that make light are called bioluminescent. More than 80 percent of animals that glow live in the deep sea. Some even live at the black depths of the ocean where sunlight cannot reach. A few glowing animals, such as fireflies and earthworms, live on the land.

PS You can see videos of bioluminescent creatures at the Monterey Institute's website.

KEYWORD PROMPTS

Monterey Institute

CREATE A RAINBOW

Would you like to make a rainbow in your home? Now you can! In this experiment, you will split a beam of light into a spectrum.

Caution: It is extremely important to never look directly at the sun because it can damage your eyes.

SUPPLIES

* baking dish or bowl with a flat bottom
* water
* small mirror
* white paper
* cooking oil
* science journal and pencil

1 Fill the dish with about 1½ inches of water. Put the mirror in the water and lean it against one side.

2 Position the dish and the mirror so that the sun shines on your mirror below the surface of the water.

3 Hold a piece of paper in front of the dish. Try to catch the sun's reflection on it. You might need to change the paper's position until you can see the rainbow colors.

4 Add a few drops of cooking oil to the water to see if that changes your rainbow. Record your observations in your science journal.

TRY THIS! Could you use a flashlight to demonstrate the separation of colors? If so, how?

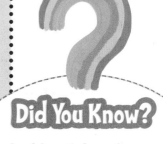

Did You Know?

A double rainbow is rare. It occurs when light rays bounce twice within a raindrop. The second rainbow is dimmer than the first because it is created with less light. When light bounces for a third time within a raindrop, a triple rainbow may appear in the sky. It is called a tertiary rainbow. In the past 250 years, there have only been five reports of a tertiary rainbow!

MAKE A SPINNING COLOR WHEEL

Our eyes see different kinds of light as color. In this activity, you are going to recombine the colors of a rainbow to make white light.

1 Lay the cardboard flat on a table. With the compass, draw a circle on the cardboard.

2 Use scissors to cut the circle out. Divide the circle into seven even pie shapes with the protractor. Color each pie shape a different rainbow color in order.

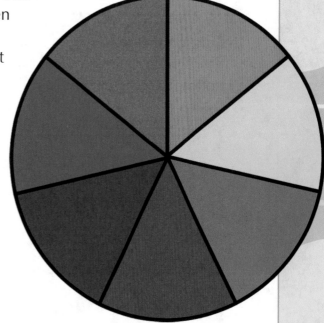

3 Poke a sharp pencil through the center of the disc to make a top.

4 Spin the disc quickly. What happens? Does the speed of your top affect your results?

TRY THIS! Make more discs, but change the order of the colors. How does this change what you see? Try using only two colors or only three colors. Record your observations in your science journal.

MAKE A SUNSET

The earth's atmosphere scatters light to create different colors. You can see light scatter here on the ground!

SUPPLIES

* tall drinking glass
* water
* whole milk
* flashlight
* science journal
* pencil

1 Fill the glass three-quarters full with water.

2 Add enough milk to make the water murky. The milk represents gas and dust particles in the atmosphere.

3 Turn the lights off and close the blinds in the room. Turn on the flashlight and aim the beam of light down directly through the bottom of the glass.

4 View the glass from different angles and observe what colors you see. Record your observations in your science journal.

TRY THIS! Add more milk and see if this changes your results.

THEN & NOW

THEN: In the past, glowing mushrooms in the woods were thought to be the work of fairies and elves.

NOW: Scientists understand how bioluminescence works. Dutch designer Daan Rooseegaarde used bioluminescent mushrooms to make city trees glow at night without using any other energy. Could these trees be the streetlights of the future?

PROJECT!

EXPERIMENT WITH LIGHT STICKS

When a glow stick is activated, the chemicals in the stick combine to produce light. In this activity, you are going to see how temperature affects the chemical reaction in a glow stick.

Caution: Never cut glow sticks open. The chemicals inside are hazardous.

1 Pour hot water into one mug and ice water into another. Activate two glow sticks according to directions on the package. Place one stick in each mug.

2 For the next 10 to 15 minutes, compare the brightness of the two sticks. Write down your observations in your science journal.

3 Repeat step 1. Place a new glow stick in each cup, but do not activate them. Leave the sticks in the cups for 5 minutes.

4 Take the sticks out and activate them. What do you notice about the glow sticks? Record your observations in your science journal.

THINK ABOUT IT: How does temperature affect the glow sticks? What does this mean for bioluminescent creatures that live in different temperatures?

EXPLORE LIGHTNING

SUPPLIES

* 2 to 3 balloons
* wool clothing, such as a wool sweater
* metal object, such as a doorknob
* science journal
* pencil

Lightning is enormously powerful. A single bolt may contain 1 billion volts of electricity! Lightning is caused by a buildup of static electricity in thunder clouds. Static electricity is made when two different objects rub together. In this experiment, you are going to make your own lightning.

1 Ask an adult to help you inflate the balloons. Set the balloons to one side. Dim the lights in a room.

2 Take a balloon and rub it vigorously over the piece of wool.

3 Position the balloon close to a metal object, such as a doorknob. Observe what happens. If nothing happens, try rubbing the balloon for a longer period. Record your observations in your science journal.

WHAT'S HAPPENING?

Rubbing the balloon against the piece of wool creates static electricity. When the balloon is placed close to the metal object, you might feel a tiny shock or see a small spark. The shock or spark is the electric charge moving from the balloon to the doorknob.

RUB

RUB

RUB

CHAPTER 3
EYE-MAZING!

• • • • • • • • • • • • • • •   • • • • • • • • • • • • • • •

Your eyes are incredible. From the moment you wake up, they work to make sense of the different shapes and colors around you. It is with your eyes that you can see the sunrise in the morning or a small frosted O in your cereal bowl. Eyes help you judge how far away objects are and how fast they might be moving toward you, such as when you take a swing at a baseball.

• •

? **INVESTIGATE!**

What do you think it was like to be the first person to see the night sky through a telescope?

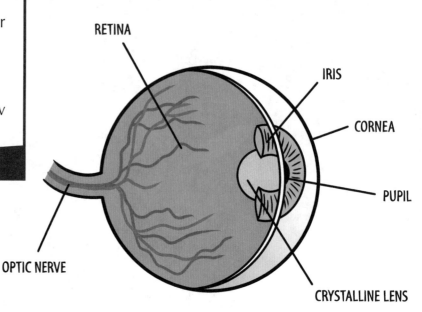

RETINA

IRIS

CORNEA

PUPIL

OPTIC NERVE

CRYSTALLINE LENS

cornea: the outermost layer of the eye.

pupil: the dark center in the middle of your eye that changes size to control how much light enters.

WORDS TO KNOW

Your eyes do not work like cameras. They do not have film or a computer chip to record the photons bouncing off objects. But eyes can detect visible light. Photons enter the front of the eye through a window called the cornea. The cornea's curved surface refracts the light rays to create an upside-down image that passes through the dark center of the eye called the pupil.

The ring of color around the pupil is the iris. The iris controls how much light can enter the pupil. Under bright conditions, the iris makes the pupil become smaller to let in less light. It makes the pupil get larger when it is darker. How does this make it easier to see?

THEN & NOW

THEN: In the thirteenth century, an unknown inventor in Italy created the first pair of eyeglasses. They were mostly worn by people who needed to be able to write things down, such as scholars or monks who copied books.

NOW: Eyeglasses are worn by people of all ages who do all kinds of things. They are constructed from newer, lightweight materials, including plastics.

Light passes through the crystalline lens of your eye, which focuses it on the retina. Inside the retina are millions of light-sensitive nerve cells. The two main types are cones and rods. The 6 million cones in a healthy eye let you see color. They only work when there is a lot of light coming into the eye. The 120 million rods are more sensitive to light than cones. The rods take over when the light is dim.

crystalline lens: the invisible lens in front of the retina that focuses light rays.

retina: the light-sensitive lining of the eyeball.

optic nerve: the part of the eye that sends messages from the retina to the brain.

WORDS TO KNOW

The retina changes the light signals into electrical signals that the optic nerve carries to your brain. Your brain translates what you are seeing, and forms the image the right way up. All of these complex steps take place in a fraction of a second!

MIRROR, MIRROR ON THE WALL

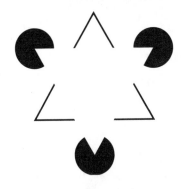

HOW MANY COMPLETE TRIANGLES DO YOU SEE?

DO YOU SEE FACES OR A VASE?

DO YOU SEE AN OLD WOMAN OR A YOUNG WOMAN?

Your eyes and brain are great partners. The brain works hard to turn light into three-dimensional images, but sometimes your eyes can trick the brain. They can make it see something that is not there. This is an optical illusion.

Optical illusions can be entertaining. They can use images, colors, and contrasts to make stationary objects look as though they are moving. Some illusions use mirrors to create strange images. When you look at an object in a mirror, light bounces off the reflection into your eyes. Depending on the shape of a mirror's surface, it can show you what is behind you or around a corner.

Mirrors in your home, such as the one in the washroom, show us what an object looks like. Mirrors used at carnivals and funhouses can make things appear upside down or even completely change their appearance. How do they do this? It isn't magic!

A mirror with a concave surface is curved away from you like the inside of a bowl. It will stretch an object out like a noodle. When you look into a concave mirror, you will look much taller and thinner than you really are.

A mirror with a convex surface is curved toward you. It bulges out like the outside of a bowl. When you look into a convex mirror you will appear much shorter and wider than you actually are. You will get a chance to experiment with these mirrors later.

CORRECTING VISION

When an eye is working normally, light particles hit the retina directly. However, not everyone's eyes work as they should.

WHAT HAS AN EYE, BUT CANNOT SEE?

HA HA HA HA HA

A sewing needle!

WORDS TO KNOW

hyperopia: when a person cannot clearly see objects that are close.

myopia: when a person cannot clearly see objects that are at a distance.

For some people, objects that are up close appear fuzzy. This condition is called farsightedness, or hyperopia. It happens when the lens cannot bend light enough to make the image clear on the retina.

What about when people can't focus on objects far away, such as a movie screen? They have shortsightedness, or myopia. Their eyes bend light so sharply that light focuses in front of the retina.

Eyeglasses and contact lenses can fix both of these conditions. They work by changing the direction of the light waves, so that the light waves hit the retina correctly and the resulting picture is clearer. A person with hyperopia needs glasses with a convex lens. A person with myopia needs glasses with a concave lens.

THE BIRTH OF THE MICROSCOPE

Before there were mirrors or lenses to focus light, people used polished stones and pools of water. In the first century CE, the Roman philosopher Seneca described how a glass bowl filled with water made letters on a page placed beneath it appear larger.

In time, people created lenses from polished glass and crystal to see things more clearly. These lenses made distant objects appear nearer and small objects appear larger.

Did You Know?

Almost 3,250 years ago, the ancient Egyptians began making glass. Scientists believe that glassmakers crushed quartz pebbles and the ashes from burned plants. They heated the mixture in a clay jar until it became a blob of glass that could then be worked into a disk of glass.

After the first eyeglasses were made in Italy, it did not take long before eyeglasses could be found all over Europe. By the sixteenth century, people had the idea to combine lenses, and the microscope was born. In the 1590s, Dutch eyeglass makers Hans and Zacharias Janssen might have built the first microscope when they combined a concave and a convex lens in a tube.

The microscope would soon be improved upon by other scientists, such as Antoni van Leeuwenhoek. His microscope could magnify objects 270 times their actual size. He used it to look at different objects, including mold and the eye of a bee.

Modern scientists use light microscopes that can magnify objects 1,000 to 2,000 times. They also use electron microscopes that bounce tiny particles called electrons off objects to magnify them up to 2 million times.

THE INVENTION OF THE TELESCOPE

In 1608, an eyeglass maker named Hans Lippershey changed the way people look at the sky. He created the first refracting telescope. A refracting telescope uses a lens at the front of the instrument to collect light and focus it. Lippershey discovered that he could make distant objects appear nearer by looking through two lenses. He placed the lenses, one convex, and one concave, in a tube. The Dutch military liked his design and became a customer.

ROBERT HOOKE

English philosopher and scientist Robert Hooke (1635–1703) was curious about insects. He used a microscope with more than one lens, called a compound microscope, to study tiny specimens such as mites, flies, and fleas. In 1665, he published his work in the book *Micrographia*. It contained incredibly detailed drawings and observations he had made with his microscope. This was the first time that most people had studied these creatures up close.

PS You can see a video about this book and look at Hooke's drawings here.

KEYWORD PROMPTS

Hooke *Micrographia* video

When news of the telescope reached Galileo, he built his own refracting telescope. It could magnify objects 15 to 20 times their actual size. In 1609, Galileo became the first person to use a telescope to study the sky. The problem with Galileo's telescope and other early refracting telescopes was that the lenses produced blurry images with colored rings around them.

In 1668, Isaac Newton found a solution to these problems. He built a reflecting telescope. Instead of a lens, Newton used a metal mirror to capture light and focus it. The resulting images were brighter and clearer as the light no longer had to travel through glass.

 INVESTIGATE!

It's time to consider and discuss: What do you think it was like to be the first person to see the night sky through a telescope?

MAKE A PERISCOPE

We can see objects because they reflect light or they produce light. But what happens when an object is around a corner? In this experiment, you are going to build a tool called a periscope that uses mirrors. The mirrors will direct the light from objects into your eyes.

1 Make a long rectangular box from the poster board. It should be about the same length as the distance from your fingertip to your elbow. The openings at either end need to be the same size as your mirrors.

2 After forming the rectangular box, secure the sides with tape.

3 At each end of the tube, cut a flap. The flaps need to be on opposite sides of the tube, and they have to be the same height as the mirror.

4 Tape a mirror to each flap.

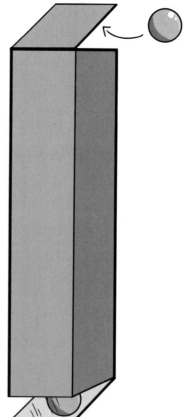

MIRROR

MIRROR

5 Experiment with tilting the mirrors. When you look through the bottom of the periscope, the bottom mirror needs to be reflecting what the top mirror is reflecting.

6 Once your periscope is working, discover what you can see over and around.

TRY THIS! How does the length of your periscope affect the image you see? Try making a new periscope that is shorter or taller than your first one. Compare your results.

HUBBLE!

In 1990, NASA launched the Hubble Space Telescope. The Hubble's two mirrors are extremely smooth, allowing them to collect incoming light and reflect and focus it. This telescope has provided astronomers with incredible images of galaxies billions of light-years away. Based on data from the Hubble, scientists have published more than 100,000 articles!

PS You can see many of the images that Hubble has taken in space.

KEYWORD PROMPTS

Hubble gallery 🔍

THE DIZZY GRID

SUPPLIES

* ✴ pencil
* ✴ ruler
* ✴ black construction paper
* ✴ scissors
* ✴ white poster board

The cones and rods in your eyes are a great team. You need both of them to see the color and detail in the world around you. Cones work best in bright light and rods in dimmer light. In this activity, you are going to discover how the rods and cones can trick the eye.

1 Measure 25 squares on the black paper. They should each be 2 inches square. Cut them out.

2 Arrange the squares in five rows across and five columns down on the bright white poster board. Use your ruler to line up the squares and leave a finger space between each square.

3 Dim the lights. Look at the center of your grid. What colors do you see? Do you notice any movement? Do you see a shape where the white lines crisscross? What happens when you stare directly at a crisscross? Repeat step 2. Turn the lights up and see how you did.

WHAT'S HAPPENING? Your eyes tell you that there are gray blinking dots where the lines crisscross. These dots are an illusion. The rods in your eyes see things in black and white. Together with the cones they make the crisscross areas darker and therefore easier to see. This makes you think that you are seeing a gray dot. When you look directly at the intersections, the blinking dot vanishes because the image falls on the part of your eye that only has cones.

TRY THIS! Look at the grid from different distances. Do you find the illusion is stronger or weaker at a certain distance? Does the illusion ever stop working?

PROJECT!

CREATE FUN HOUSE MIRRORS

A favorite boardwalk attraction is a funhouse where people can laugh at their wiggly figures in the mirrors. You can create curved mirrors at home. This experiment works best if you have a small group to join in.

SUPPLIES

* ✳ 1–2 rolls of reflective wrapping paper or Mylar
* ✳ ruler
* ✳ pencil
* ✳ scissors
* ✳ science journal
* ✳ masking or double-sided tape

1 Cut out an 8½-by-11 piece of reflective paper. Hold it up in front of you and observe what happens to your image when the paper is flat, curved inward, and curved outward. Record your results in your science journal.

2 Based on your observations from step 1, create a hall of fun mirrors. Using the ruler, measure and cut out the reflective paper into rectangles of various sizes. One should be long enough to reflect your entire body.

3 Position your mirrors along a hallway. Before you attach the paper mirrors to the wall, curve some of them outward and some of them inward. Secure the paper with tape on the back.

4 Invite friends to check out your funhouse! What kinds of funny shapes do you see?

TRY THIS! Cut the paper into other shapes, such as a zigzag. Observe what happens to your reflection.

CREATE A MAGNIFYING GLASS

A magnifying glass is used to make objects appear larger than they really are. Once larger, they are easier for people to see. The ancient Egyptians used pieces of a shiny stone called obsidian to look at small objects. Today, plastic is often used to make simple magnifying glasses. You are going to discover if water can be used to magnify objects.

1 Peel the paper off the twist tie. Make a loop with the wire.

2 Take the wire loop and dip it into the glass of water. The loop needs to fill with water.

3 Hold the wire loop over the newsprint and read the letters through the water.

THINGS TO NOTICE: What do you notice about the size of the letters through the water? Have you created a convex or concave lens? Explain your answer. Alter the size of the loop and see if this changes your results.

TRY THIS! Use other fluids in the magnifying glass. Try juice, milk, tea, and other drinks. Which works best? Why?

Did You Know?

In ancient Rome, a writer called Seneca discovered that he could make tiny letters larger. What was his secret? Seneca looked at letters through a glass bowl filled with water. The water-filled bowl worked just like a convex lens, making the letters appear larger.

PROJECT!

FIND YOUR BLIND SPOT

You have read that your eye has millions of light-sensitive nerve cells. But did you know that there is an area of the retina that has no rod or cone cells? It is called a blind spot. If an object falls into this area, it cannot be seen. Usually, we do not notice our blind spot because the brain patches the image together. In this experiment, you are going to discover where your blind spot is.

SUPPLIES
* strip of paper about the length of a cellular phone
* black marker

1 Draw a small dot at one end of the paper and a small letter t at the other end.

2 Hold the paper in your hands at arms distance.

3 Close your left eye. Look at the dot with your right eye. Slowly move the paper closer to you until you can no longer see the small letter t. This is your blind spot. Repeat this experiment for your other eye.

THINK ABOUT IT: Usually we don't even notice our blind spots because we have two eyes working together and a brain that is very good at guessing. What are some scenarios in which having a blind spot can be a problem? Can you think of ways people can avoid getting into trouble because of a blind spot?

CHAPTER 4
OP-TECH

We depend on light technology. It makes our life easier. With a flip of a switch, light fills your bedroom. With a swipe of your finger, you can make a phone call with your smartphone. Some gadgets make our lives easier and safer and some make our lives more fun. In the hands of doctors, light technology can be used to treat patients. Optics make it possible for us to take digital pictures and watch our favorite television programs.

Does you house or school use solar power? The sun produces a huge amount of energy. Each day, the earth receives more solar energy than the earth's entire population uses in a single year!

? INVESTIGATE!

What do you use every day that requires light?

Solar energy is an important renewable energy source that won't run out for billions of years. We can use solar energy to replace fossil fuels such as coal or oil. Fossil fuels formed hundreds of millions of years ago and cannot be replaced. Most experts believe that fossil fuels harm the environment when they are burned for energy. This is why solar energy is important.

renewable energy: a form of energy that doesn't get used up, including the energy of the sun and the wind.

fossil fuels: coal, oil, and natural gas. These non-renewable energy sources come from the fossils of plants and tiny animals that lived millions of years ago.

photovoltaic: technology used to convert sunlight into electricity.

electron: a particle in an atom with a negative charge.

WORDS TO KNOW

How do we change energy from the sun into energy we can use in our homes? One of the most popular ways to collect the sun's energy is with solar photovoltaic panels. Photovoltaic panels take energy from the sun and change it into electricity. This change takes place in the tiny solar cells on the panels.

Electricity is energy created by the movement of electrons between atoms. Each cell in the solar panel has two separate layers, like a sandwich. The first layer is packed with electrons.

THEN & NOW

THEN: During the Stone Age, people made light by filling the hollows of shells and rocks with animal fat and a wick made from grass and set it alight.

NOW: People light their homes with LED bulbs that can produce light for 50,000 to 100,000 hours.

When sunlight hits this layer, electrons jump to the second layer, which in turn makes more electrons jump. The continual movement of electrons generates electricity.

Deserts are popular locations for solar power plants because they are bombarded with direct sunlight. The Mojave Desert, in the southwestern United States, experiences more than 300 days of sunshine a year. Two of the world's largest solar plants, Desert Sunlight and Topaz Solar Farm, are found here. Together, their millions of solar panels produce energy for about 340,000 homes.

WHY DID THE GARDENER PLANT A LIGHT BULB?

HA HA HA HA HA

To grow a power plant.

SOLAR CARS

Solar panels are used for more than generating electricity for homes. Hand-held calculators, spacecraft, and cars also use solar panels to generate power.

If you saw a solar car, you might think it looked like a spaceship. Most solar cars are quite flat in order to maximize the amount of sunlight that hits them. Silicon cells on the cars convert sunlight into usable energy. The energy then charges batteries that power the car's engine, lights, and other systems.

AND THEY'RE OFF!

A team of students at Stanford University is up for the challenge of designing solar cars. The school is home to the top solar car team in the United States. Their solar car has raced in solar-powered competitions all over the world, including a race across the Australian Outback. The World Solar Challenge has solar cars race a grueling 2,000 miles from Darwin to Adelaide. **Learn more about the Stanford team here.**

KEYWORD PROMPTS

solar car Stanford 🔍

There are several challenges to building a car that can harvest and store solar power. The car's batteries take up a lot of space. Plus, solar cars get very hot, so air conditioning is essential.

THE LIGHT BULB

Flip on a switch. Electric lights are all around you. But it wasn't always this way. Beginning in the early 1800s, inventors worked to convert electricity into light. In 1878, Joseph Wilson Swan of Britain invented a light bulb that used a carbon paper filament.

The bulb glowed, but only for a short period. A year later, Thomas Edison and his team of inventors succeeded in using a carbonized piece of thread as a filament. Their incandescent light bulb burned for more than 14 hours!

WORDS TO KNOW

filament: a very fine wire or thread. In an electric bulb, the filament glows when heated by a current.

incandescent: a source of electric light that works by heating a filament.

61

phosphors: a material that glows.

diode: an electronic part that limits the flow of current to one direction.

WORDS TO KNOW

FILAMENT

INCANDESCENT LIGHT BULB

Edison kept experimenting. He found that a filament made from bamboo was even better. It allowed bulbs to glow for more than 1,200 hours!

While incandescent bulbs provided people with light, they were not energy efficient. In the 1930s, researchers began coating long glass tubes with phosphors. This way, inventors made florescent lamps that burned at lower temperatures and were more energy efficient.

SPIRAL TUBING

It wasn't until the late 1970s that engineers shrank long florescent tubes down into small coiled bulbs, or compact florescent lights (CFLs). CFLs last longer than traditional bulbs and use 70 percent less energy.

PHOSPHORS COATING

As the traditional light bulbs burn out in your home, you might replace them with CFL bulbs. You might use an even more energy-efficient light-emitting diode (LED). An LED is a type of diode that electricity flows through to produce light. LEDs are part of many inventions, from computers and televisions to traffic signals and cars.

CFL BULB

FIBER OPTICS

How does an email travel around the world? Telephone messages, videos, and emails can travel as coded pulses of light through thin glass or plastic tubes called optical fibers. The tubes are more like threads, no larger than a human hair.

If you shine light down a regular tube, it escapes out the end and bounces off whatever object is in its path. Optical fibers have reflective walls. This keeps the light inside.

There are 1.2 billion miles of optical fibers laid down all around the world. They are able to carry more data than traditional copper cables. Some fiber optic systems are capable of sending 1,000 books a second! Fiber optics are also used in medicine. A tool called an endoscope uses fiber optics. It has a light at one end and sometimes a digital camera that allows doctors to see clearly during surgery or to make diagnoses.

MEET A LIGHT PIONEER!

CHARLES K. KAO

Electrical engineer and physicist, Charles K. Kao (1933–) was born in Shanghai, China. When he began working in the field of telecommunications in the 1960s, telephones were just becoming popular. In 1966, Kao published a paper explaining that light in optical fibers could be used for communication across long distances. His discovery revolutionized telecommunications.

acronym: a word that is formed from the first letters in each word of a phrase. The word *laser* is an example.

WORDS TO KNOW

WHAT IS A LASER?

A laser is a device that creates a powerful beam of light. The word *laser* is an acronym. It stands for, "**l**ight **a**mplification by **s**timulated **e**mission of **r**adiation." It's pretty easy to see why people commonly use the word *laser* instead.

Light from a laser is unique. Unlike sunlight, which spreads out in many directions, light from a laser travels in tight waves that are all the same size.

DID YOU KNOW LASER IS AN ACRONYM? *LIGHT AMPLIFICATION BY STIMULATED EMISSION OF RADIATION!*

WOW. NO WONDER THEY JUST CALL IT A "LASER."

BEEP

SUNLIGHT

LASER LIGHT

People have found many exciting uses for lasers. Surgeons use them to operate on eyes. Lasers read data stored in barcodes. Some lasers can cut through metal and fabric. In astronomy, powerful lasers help astronomers to see more clearly.

The earth's atmosphere bends light in many different directions, causing the planets and stars to shimmer. This isn't good for astronomers! They want to see things in space clearly. The problem can be corrected by shining a laser into the atmosphere to create an artificial star. The light from this fake star is used to correct the telescopes' mirrors, and the result is sharper images of the real stars.

THE FUTURE IS HERE!

A cloak that can make a person invisible isn't just in stories anymore. Researchers at the University of Rochester have created a device that hides objects by bending light around them. This device might help with blind spots in vehicles or allow surgeons to see through their own hands.

Another group of scientists created a box painted with special, light-scattering paint that makes it invisible. Other researchers made a cloak that hides things by creating a much higher temperature that bends light away from the wearer! These are exciting developments, though there is still a lot of work to be done before they are useful.

? INVESTIGATE!

It's time to consider and discuss: What do you use every day that requires light?

65

ACRONYM JUMBLE

You have learned that the word *laser* is an acronym. In this fun game, make up acronyms for your friends to solve.

SUPPLIES

* paper
* pencil
* 2 to 4 friends or classmates

1 Select one person to create the acronym. You will be taking turns in this game. Be certain that everyone in your small group has a chance to create and solve an acronym.

2 The person who is "it" thinks of a sentence about light. They can choose one from this book or think of their own.

3 Create an acronym for the sentence and write it on a piece of paper, making sure that no one can see it until they're ready to share it.

4 Each player takes a turn guessing what the acronym stands for.

5 The person who solves the acronym becomes the "it" person in the next round.

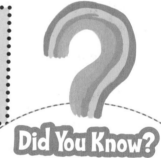

Did You Know?

Holograms create ghostly images when they are moved back and forth. You've probably seen them on paper money, credit cards, and toys. A laser creates these three-dimensional photographs. A piece of glass coated in silver splits the laser beam in half as it is being shone at a piece of photographic film. When the two beams come together again on the piece of film, they produce a hologram.

WORDS TO KNOW

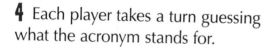

hologram: a special kind of picture produced by a laser that looks three-dimensional.

THE SUN VERSUS A LAMP

Is the sun or a lamp more effective at heating up a jug of water? Let's find out in this experiment!

SUPPLIES

* science journal and pencil
* 2 clear jugs of tap water
* thermometer

1 Which will heat up faster, the jug of water placed in the sun or the jug of water placed under a lamp? In your science journal, write down your hypothesis.

2 Take a temperature reading of each jug of water. Record the temperature in your journal.

3 Place one jug in a sunny spot outside and one under a lamp. The lamp's light needs to shine directly on the water. A study lamp with a flexible neck works best.

4 Take the temperature of the water every 10 minutes for 1 hour. Record your observations in your science journal.

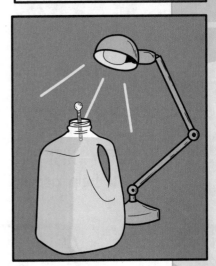

5 After 1 hour, compare your results. Was your prediction correct? What do your results tell you about energy from the sun and energy from a lamp?

TRY THIS! Graph your results. You can use this site to help: nces.ed.gov/nceskids/createagraph.

ICE HOT

In this experiment, you will investigate how color affects the way heat is absorbed.

1 Place the ice-cube tray on a flat surface. Pour water into each of the sections, leaving a little room for the food coloring.

2 Add a drop or two of food coloring to each section. Make lots of different colors.

3 Carefully place the tray in the freezer and leave it there until the water turns to ice.

4 In your science journal, predict which color ice cubes will melt faster.

5 Place the ice cubes on the baking tray and set it out in direct sunlight.

6 Write down your observations. Were your predictions correct?

TRY THIS! Put your results into a line graph. You can use this site to help: nces.ed.gov/nceskids/createagraph.

PROJECT!

TEA TIME

In this experiment, you are going to discover how the sun's heat can be used to cook. Your results may vary depending on how sunny the day is.

SUPPLIES

* science journal and pencil
* 2 mason jars
* 2 tea bags
* water
* kettle

Caution: Have an adult help you with the boiling water. If your tea bags do not have strings, use a spoon to remove them.

1 Do you think the tea made with solar energy will look, taste, and smell the same as tea made with boiling water? Write down your prediction in your science journal.

2 Place a tea bag in each mason jar.

3 Fill one of the mason jars with tap water and place it in direct sunlight for 2 to 3 hours. When the solar tea turns a deep amber color, remove the tea bag and dispose of it.

4 Ask an adult to fill the other mason jar with boiling water. When the tea becomes the same color as the sun tea, remove the tea bag and dispose of it.

5 Compare the teas. Do they look, taste, and smell the same? Explain why they are the same or different. Do you think your results would change at different times of the year? Explain your answer.

CHAPTER 5
CREATE WITH LIGHT

Light has always inspired people. Curiosity about how light behaves has encouraged the discovery and creation of many forms of visual art.

In the nineteenth century, audiences were awed by the first still images produced by photography. Later, they were caught up in the excitement of moving pictures. Artists have also used light to create objects of beauty. These include carved windows, colored glass, and paintings that show scenes from their imagination, books, and everyday life.

? INVESTIGATE!

What are some ways people use light to make art and technology?

Impressionist: an artist who uses dabs or strokes of color to look like actual reflected light.

WORDS TO KNOW

Throughout history, people have tried to capture color and light with paint. Some nineteenth-century artists became known for the way they used natural light in their paintings. They were called the Impressionists. The Impressionists created canvases that were fresh and filled with light.

They preferred to paint outdoors and capture scenes using bright colors. The paint was applied directly to the canvas in rapid brush strokes. Instead of traditional subjects from myths or the Bible, they painted everyday people and scenes. Artists who belonged to this group included Claude Monet, Auguste Renoir, and Edgar Degas.

WHERE DOES BAD LIGHT GO?

HA HA HA HA HA

To prism!

When the work of the Impressionists was first shown, many people were critical. They thought the paintings seemed unfinished. With time, these artists and their work became more accepted. They sold their paintings and became successful. Now, many Impressionist paintings hang in museums all over the world.

PS

You can see the work of the Impressionists here. How does the artist capture sunlight and water? How does the artist make you think the clouds are moving or the sun is shining?

KEYWORD PROMPTS

National Gallery Art Impressionism

STAINED GLASS

Few things are more dazzling to the eye than the kaleidoscope of colors in stained glass windows. Stained glass has been used to create beautiful patterns for more than 1,000 years. It became popular in Europe during the Gothic Period and during the Renaissance.

To make stained glass, artisans first had to make glass by heating up sand and other minerals. People learned they could add color to the glass by using different materials—for example, cobalt for blue and iron for green.

Artists used the colored glass as if it was paint. They placed colored glass on top of a design. Then, they fitted lead strips around each section. Additional details, such as shading or facial features, were added to the glass surface with paint. The stained glass was used in windows.

In churches, the stained glass windows let in light and represented God and illustrated Bible stories. Presenting Bible stories in picture form was important because most people could not read hundreds of years ago.

SAVING STAINED GLASS

The Sainte-Chapelle chapel in Paris has some of the most famous stained glass in the world. The chapel's 6,458 square feet of stained glass windows are from the thirteenth century. Due to fire, pollution, and age, over time the windows became damaged. For seven years, restorers worked on the windows using tiny lasers to bring them back to their original glory.

PS You can watch a short video on the restoration of the windows here.

KEYWORD PROMPTS

centre des monuments nationaux sainte chapelle

THE CAMERA

Photography is a fun way to express yourself, create art, and record important events. With the invention of the camera phone, taking a picture has never been easier. But it wasn't always this way!

First came the camera obscura. This "camera" was a wooden box with a lens. The lens at the front projected an upside down image onto a mirror. The mirror flipped the image the right way up and onto a viewing plate. Artists then could copy the picture by hand.

WORDS TO KNOW

camera obscura: a box with a convex lens used for projecting an image onto a flat surface.

73

WORDS TO KNOW

heliography: a process using sunlight to recreate permanent images.

daguerreotype: a process used to produce photographs on thin metal plates.

Scientist and inventor Joseph Niépce of France wanted to capture images with light. In the early 1800s, he tried reproducing pictures on metal plates with chemicals that reacted to sunlight. He called his method heliography, or sun drawing. In 1822, after exposing one of these plates to light for eight hours, he succeeded!

In 1839, fellow Frenchman Louis Daguerre invented a way of processing photographs on thin sheets of metal in less than 30 minutes. He called his process the daguerreotype. Within a few years of his discovery, daguerreotype studios began popping up all over Europe and North America. At the same time, an English member of parliament and inventor William Henry Fox Talbot found a way to print photographs on paper.

Less than 50 years later, photography was no longer just for professional studios. In 1888, an American named George Eastman created the first popular camera. His company, Kodak, had a catchy slogan: "You press the button—we do the rest."

Did You Know?

The world's first photograph was of the view from the window of the home of Joseph Niépce. To see the first photograph and learn more, go to this website.

PS

KEYWORD PROMPTS

Harry Ransom Center first photograph 🔍

sensor: a device that is sensitive to light.

pixels: the small dots that make up a digital image.

WORDS TO KNOW

Today, the digital camera has largely replaced the film camera. A digital camera doesn't use film. It changes light into digital signals.

Light enters through the lens and is focused onto a sensor. The image is broken up into millions of tiny squares, called pixels, that cover the sensor. The color and brightness of each pixel is stored as a number. Images can then be displayed on a computer or other device. They can be shared, downloaded, or printed.

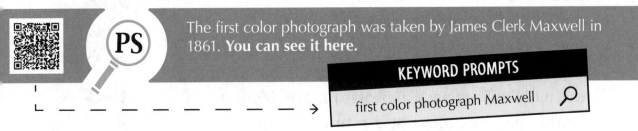

PS

The first color photograph was taken by James Clerk Maxwell in 1861. **You can see it here.**

KEYWORD PROMPTS

first color photograph Maxwell

MOVING PICTURES

In 1891, Thomas Edison found a way to make pictures move. He called his invention the Kinetoscope. It looked like a large wooden box, but at the top was a peephole. Only one person at a time could look inside. When they did, a small motor carried images on film past a magnifying glass. They moved just fast enough to make them look as if the pictures were moving. One of Edison's first films was of a man sneezing!

PS You can watch Edison's films and other early movies here.

KEYWORD PROMPTS

Edison Company motion picture video 🔍

Two French brothers, Louis and Auguste Lumière, were fascinated with the inventions of Thomas Edison. In 1895, they created a machine that could project images onto a screen. They called their motion picture camera the Cinématographe. It played images at 16 frames a second, making the individual images appear to move. Modern motion pictures move at a rate of 30 frames a second!

MEET A LIGHT PIONEER!

PHILO T. FARNSWORTH (1906–1971)

Inventor Philo T. Farnsworth was still in high school when he became interested in electricity. At the age of 14, he explained to a teacher that he thought it was possible to change electricity into pictures. His idea was to control the speed and direction of the electrons. In 1927, Farnsworth successfully produced an image on a television. Today, he is recognized as the "Father of Television."

OPTICS AROUND YOU

Our world is packed with examples of technology that use light. Thanks to lasers, it is possible to create running shoes with a 3-D printer. The same printer can be used to make tools, clothing, toys, and prosthetic limbs.

Examples of light-based technology found in your home and school include television sets, printers, and scanners. In your backpack there might be a mobile phone or bank card. As you have learned, there are also examples found in hospitals, spacecraft, and movie theaters.

WHAT DO YOU GET IF YOU CROSS A CAMERA WITH A MIRROR?

HA HA HA HA HA

A camera that takes selfies!

The ancient Greeks used light to communicate. Greek soldiers used their shields to send coded messages. They flashed signals back and forth with their shields. We no longer need shields to send messages, but we still use light in the form of fiber optics to communicate.

Each year, scientists and engineers design new applications for light in fields from medicine to astronomy. There are many possibilities for incorporating optics into our lives. What invention will scientists create next? No one knows, but maybe you will be the person to make the next discovery!

? INVESTIGATE!

It's time to consider and discuss:
What are some ways people use light to make art and technology?

SUPPLIES

* science journal and pencil
* watercolor paint
* brushes, 1 large and 1 medium
* cup of water
* paper towel
* 11-by-15-inch watercolor paper

PROJECT!

SKY PAINTING

Impressionists watched as the light changed throughout the day. They used color to express these changes and moods. You are going to use watercolor paint to create three sky paintings that capture a specific time of day.

Caution: Remember to never look directly at the sun!

1 Observe the sky at three different times of the day—morning, noon, and dusk. In your science journal, write down what colors you see, the location of the sun and clouds, and weather conditions. You can organize your data in a chart like the one shown below.

Time	Colors	Sun and Clouds	Weather
Morning	pink and orange	sun just rising, clear skies	rained last night
Noon			
Dusk			

2 Divide your watercolor paper into three sections for three individual paintings. You want to mix up the order of time, such as dusk, then morning, then noon. Create a wash that reflects a specific time of day. A wash is when an artist paints over an entire section or sheet. To make a wash, dip your large brush in water and sweep it over the entire section to wet it. The paper needs to be damp, but not soaking wet.

3 Paint over each section in the colors that reflect this time. Repeat this step for each section of paper.

Did You Know?

Each evening at 8 pm, music, fireworks, and lasers light up the skies and buildings of Hong Kong's Victoria Harbor. The *Guinness Book of World Records* lists the show as the largest permanent sound and light show in the world. One show illuminates more than 40 buildings around the harbor to show Hong Kong's growth.

4 When the paper has dried, ask your friends if they can tell which painting represents morning, which painting represents noon, and which painting represents dusk.

THINK ABOUT IT: Does the mood of your paintings change or stay the same for each time of day? Is there anything you would change about your paintings to better communicate the time of day? If so, explain what you would do and try again.

CREATE A PHOTO EXHIBIT

In this activity, you will photograph objects from different angles and in different lights. You will discover how artists use light and shadow to emphasize details or contrasts in their works.

1 Collect three objects of different textures and materials. Place the objects on a flat work surface.

2 Using a light source, select one object at a time to photograph.

3 When you are pleased with your arrangement, take three photos of the same object from the front, side, and up close. Repeat this step for all three objects.

PROJECT!

4 Print out your photographs. Look at them and sort them first by object. Next, sort them based on the light source. Last, base them on how the object was photographed. What do you notice?

THEN: On June 19, 1905, the first public movie house, named the Nickelodeon, opened in the United States.

NOW: There are more than 40,000,000 movie screens in the United States.

5 Decide how you are going to present your photographs and glue them to the craft paper. Invite your friends or family to look at them. Can they guess where you were standing when you snapped each photograph? Can they guess what the light source was? You can explain to them how you created and organized your photographs.

THINK ABOUT IT: Have you ever wondered how animals see the world? Cats are able to see better at night than people because they have more rods in their eyes. Birds are able to see ultraviolet light because they have one more color-sensitive cone than humans. The mantis shrimp has an incredible 12 different color-sensitive cells! With the help of an adult, research one animal online. Investigate how its eyesight compares to humans. Try to take a photo of your objects from the viewpoint of this animal. Add or take away color and detail based on your research.

PS You can learn about the eyes of many different animals here.

KEYWORD PROMPTS

National Geographic animal eyes

WORD GAME

Use words from the glossary and text to create a silly story. After you have finished filling in the blank lines, read your story to a friend.

- noun: a person, place, or thing.

- plural noun: more than one person, place, or thing.

- adjective: a word that describes a noun.

- verb: an action word.

- adverb: a word that describes a verb. Many adverbs end in -ly.

Over the summer, I _____ at the local pet store. I was in charge of
<small>VERB</small>
_____ and taking pet photographs. I loved taking pictures of the
<small>VERB</small>
_____ and the _____. _____, I took the
<small>ADJECTIVE</small>   <small>NOUN</small>   <small>NOUN</small>   <small>ADVERB</small>
pets across the road to the park. I liked taking photos first thing in the
morning, when the sun was _____ in the sky. The sky was always
<small>ADJECTIVE</small>
different shades of _____. I also liked taking shots at the end of the
<small>COLOR</small>
day, when the sun was _____. The sky looked like _____. It
<small>ADJECTIVE</small>   <small>NOUN</small>
had _____ and _____ in it.
<small>NOUN</small>   <small>NOUN</small>

The _____ time of the day to take a photo was noon. The sun was
<small>ADJECTIVE</small>
too _____. I had to _____ for shade under _____ or by
<small>ADJECTIVE</small>   <small>VERB</small>   <small>NOUN</small>
the _____.
<small>NOUN</small>

Today, a friend of my brother _____ in a _____ for me to
<small>VERB</small>   <small>NOUN</small>
photograph. I was _____ surprised. I had never been asked to
<small>ADVERB</small>
photograph a _____ pet before. Before I could _____ the photo,
<small>NOUN</small>   <small>VERB</small>
the _____ _____ away!
<small>NOUN</small>   <small>VERB</small>

A

aether: an unknown material that some people once believed filled space.

acronym: a word that is formed from the first letters in each word of a phrase. The word *laser* is an example.

atmosphere: the blanket of air surrounding the earth.

aurora australis: The southern lights.

aurora borealis: The northern lights.

aurora: a natural display of shimmering light and color in the night sky.

Aztecs: a Native American people who established an empire in central Mexico.

B

BCE: put after a date, BCE stands for Before Common Era and counts years down to zero. CE stands for Common Era and counts years up from zero. This book was published in 2016 CE.

bioluminescent: when living things give off light by hosting a chemical reaction in their bodies.

C

camera obscura: a box with a convex lens used for projecting an image onto a flat surface.

chariot: a vehicle pulled by horses used by ancient Greeks and Romans for races and in battle.

climate: the average weather patterns in an area during a long period of time.

concave: curved inward like the inside of a bowl or a cave.

condensation: the process of a gas cooling down and changing into a liquid.

convex: curved outward like the outside of a bowl.

cornea: the outermost layer of the eye.

crystalline lens: the invisible lens in front of the retina that focuses light rays.

culture: the beliefs and behavior of a particular group of people.

D

daguerreotype: a process used to produce photographs on thin metal plates.

diode: an electronic part that limits the flow of current to one direction.

E

eclipse: when a planet or other body in space is hidden by another body in space.

electricity: a form of energy that results from the interaction of electrically charged particles.

electromagnetic: one of the fundamental forces of the universe, which is responsible for magnetic attraction and electrical charges.

electromagnetic spectrum: the entire range of electromagnetic waves.

electron: a particle in an atom with a negative charge.

element: a pure substance whose atoms are all the same. It cannot be broken down into a simpler substance. Everything in the universe is made up of elements and combinations of elements. Oxygen, gold, hydrogen, and helium are elements.

evaporation: the process of a liquid heating up and changing into a gas, such as water vapor.

F

filament: a very fine wire or thread. In an electric bulb the filament glows when heated by a current.

fossil fuels: coal, oil, and natural gas. These non-renewable energy sources come from the fossils of plants and tiny animals that lived millions of years ago.

G

gamma ray: short electromagnetic waves.

Gothic Period: a period of time from the twelfth to sixteenth centuries. A style of architecture that features pointed arches was popular during the Gothic period.

gravity: a physical force that pulls objects toward the center of the earth.

H

Haida: a native group of people living mostly in the Pacific Northeast.

heliography: a process using sunlight to recreate permanent images.

hologram: a special kind of picture produced by a laser that looks three-dimensional.

hyperopia: when a person cannot clearly see objects that are close.

I

illuminated: describes an object that can reflect light to our eyes.

Impressionist: an artist who uses dabs or strokes of color to look like actual reflected light.

incandescent: a source of electric light that works by heating a filament.

infrared: an invisible type of light with a longer wavelength than visible light, which can also be felt as heat.

L

legend: a story that is partly based on a true historical event or person.

lens: a piece of curved glass that can bend light to form an image that appears larger or smaller than the original object.

luminous: describes an object that gives out its own light.

M

magnetism: the attracting and repelling force that results from the motion of electrically charged particles.

magnetosphere: an area in space around the earth that is controlled by the earth's magnetic field.

microwave: an electromagnetic wave that we use to heat food.

mirage: something that is not as it seems, such as when a distant object is seen inverted by reflection and distorted.

molecule: a very small particle made of combinations of atoms.

myopia: when a person cannot clearly see objects that are at a distance.

myth: a story about make-believe creatures that people once believed were real.

N

Norse: people who lived in ancient Scandinavia.

O

obelisk: a four-sided tapered stone tower.

optical fiber: glass or plastic threads that transmit information in the form of light.

optical illusion: a trick of the eyes that makes people see something differently than it really is.

optic nerve: the part of the eye that sends messages from the retina to the brain.

optics: the science of visible and invisible light.

P

particle: a very tiny part of something.

pharaoh: the title for an ancient Egyptian king.

phosphors: a material that glows.

photon: a particle of light that travels in waves.

photosynthesis: the process in which plants use light energy, carbon dioxide, and water to produce glucose and oxygen.

photovoltaic: technology used to convert sunlight into electricity.

pixels: the small dots that make up a digital image.

precipitation: water in the air in any form, such as snow, hail, or rain, that falls to the ground.

prism: a solid, often made of glass, that is used to split light.

properties: the unique characteristics of something.

prosthetic: relating to an artificial body part.

pupil: the dark center in the middle of your eye that changes size to control how much light enters.

Q

quantum physics: an area of physics founded on the idea that light energy is made of different packets of energy.

R

radio wave: an electromagnetic wave used to transmit radio and television signals and for navigation.

reflection: when light hits an object and bounces off it.

refraction: when the direction of light changes.

Renaissance: a creative period of time in Europe, from the fourteenth to seventeenth centuries.

renewable energy: a form of energy that doesn't get used up, including the energy of the sun and the wind.

retina: the light-sensitive lining of the eyeball.

S

Scandinavia: the countries of Sweden, Norway, Denmark, and Finland.

sensor: a device that is sensitive to light.

shadow: a dark area created when light is blocked by an object.

solar wind: a flow of electrically charged particles from the sun.

spectrum: in optics, a separation of color.

speed of light: the speed at which light travels, which is 186,000 miles per second.

supernatural: beings, objects, or events that cannot be explained.

T

transpiration: the process by which a plant pulls water up through its roots, which then collects on its leaves and evaporates into the atmosphere.

U

ultraviolet: a kind of light with short wavelengths. It can't be seen with the naked eye.

X

X-rays: radiation that allows doctors to see your bones.

METRIC CONVERSIONS

Use this chart to find the metric equivalents to the English measurements in this book. If you need to know a half measurement, divide by two. If you need to know twice the measurement, multiply by two. How do you find a quarter measurement? How do you find three times the measurement?

English	Metric
1 inch	2.5 centimeters
1 foot	30.5 centimeters
1 yard	0.9 meter
1 mile	1.6 kilometers
1 pound	0.5 kilogram
1 teaspoon	5 milliliters
1 tablespoon	15 milliliters
1 cup	237 milliliters

WEBSITES

MIKIDS.com Simple Machines:
mikids.com/Smachines.htm

BBC Bitesize: Light:
bbc.co.uk/bitesize/ks2/science/physical_processes/light/read/1

International Year of Light:
light2015.org

Exploratorium:
exploratorium.edu/snacks

Light Science for Kids:
interior-deluxe.com/light-science-for-kids.html

Optics 4 Kids:
optics4kids.org

SPIE:
spie.org/education/education-outreach-resources/hands-on-optics

Stanford Solar Center:
solar-center.stanford.edu

BOOKS

A Kid's Book of Experiments with Light (Surprising Science Experiments). Gardner, Robert. Enslow Publishing, 2016.

A Project Guide to Light and Optics (Physical Science Projects for Kids). Kessler, Colleen. Mitchell Lane Publishers, 2011.

Experiments in Light and Sound with Toys and Everyday Stuff (Fun Science). Rompella, Natalie. Capstone Press, 2015.

Eye: How It Works. Macaulay, David. David Macaulay Studio, 2013.

Eye to Eye: How Animals See the World. Jenkins, Steve. HMH Books for Young Readers, 2014.

Hands-On Science: Sound and Light. Challoner, Jack. Kingfisher, 2013.

Playing With Light and Shadows (First Step Nonfiction: Light and Sound). Boothroyd, Jennifer. Lerner, 2014.

Tabletop Scientist—The Science of Light: Projects and Experiments with Light and Color. Parker, Steve. Dover Publications, 2013.

QR CODE GLOSSARY

Page 5: ibnalhaytham.com

Page 7: phys.org/news/2015-03-particle.html

Page 14: timeanddate.com

Page 20: whc.unesco.org/en/list/246/video

Page 25: teacher.scholastic.com/writewit/mff/myths.htm

Page 25: americanfolklore.net/folklore/myths-legends

Page 33: newtonproject.sussex.ac.uk/prism.php?id=1

Page 37: nasa.gov/mission_pages/sunearth/aurora-videos/index.html

Page 39: montereyinstitute.org/noaa/lesson06/l6la2.htm

Page 51: youtube.com/watch?v=pWk0cNAnC0c

Page 53: hubblesite.org/gallery

Page 61: solarcar.stanford.edu

Page 71: nga.gov/collection/gallery/gg86/gg86-main1.html

Page 73: youtube.com/watch?v=PM-2Plu-DYc

Page 74: hrc.utexas.edu/exhibitions/permanent/firstphotograph/kids/#top

Page 75: nationalgeographic.com/wallpaper/photography/
photos/milestones-photography/color-tartan-ribbon/

Page 76: loc.gov/collection/edison-company-motion-pictures-
and-sound-recordings/about-this-collection

Page 81: ngm.nationalgeographic.com/2016/02/evolution-of-eyes-text

ESSENTIAL QUESTIONS

Introduction: How do you think the ancient Greeks explained why people could not see in the dark?

Chapter 1: How did ancient cultures show the importance of the sun to their survival? How do today's cultures show this?

Chapter 2: If light contains all colors, then why does a blue bike look blue?

Chapter 3: What do you think it was like to be the first person to see the night sky through a telescope?

Chapter 4: What do you use every day that requires light?

Chapter 5: What are some ways people use light to make art and technology?